Mako Sharks

BY ALLAN MOREY

AMICUS HIGH INTEREST • AMICUS INK

Amicus High Interest and Amicus Ink are imprints of Amicus
P.O. Box 1329, Mankato, MN 56002
www.amicuspublishing.us

Library of Congress Cataloging-in-Publication Data
Morey, Allan, author.
Mako sharks / by Allan Morey.
 pages cm. – (Sharks)
Audience: K to grade 3.
Includes bibliographical references and index.
 ISBN 978-1-60753-979-7 (library binding) –
 ISBN 978-1-68152-092-6 (pbk.) –
 ISBN 978-1-68151-013-2 (ebook)
1. Mako sharks–Juvenile literature. 2. Sharks–Juvenile
literature. I. Title.
QL638.95.L3M67 2017
597.3'3–dc23
                                    2015033751

Editor: Wendy Dieker
Series Designer: Kathleen Petelinsek
Book Designer: Aubrey Harper
Photo Researcher: Rebecca Bernin

Photo Credits: wildestanimal/Getty cover; Andy Murch/Visuals
Unlimited/Corbis 5; Andy Murch/OceanwideImages.com 6;
Andy Murch/OceanwideImages.com 8-9; kan_khampanya/
Shutterstock 10; Willyam Bradberry/Shutterstock 13; Charles
Hood/Alamy 14; Greg Amptman/123rf 17; Kike Calvo/
Getty 18; Greg Amptman/Shutterstock 20-21; BryanToro/
iStock 22; Ronald C. Modra/Sports Imagery/Getty 25;
Minden Pictures/Minden Pictures/Superstock 26; Andy Murch/
OceanwideImages.com 29

Printed in the United States of America.

HC 10 9 8 7 6 5 4 3 2 1
PB 10 9 8 7 6 5 4 3 2 1

Table of Contents

Shark Speedsters

A school of fish moves through the ocean. The fish dart left. Then they swim to the right. They are on the look out for danger.

But the fish do not see the mako shark lurking below. In the blink of an eye, it shoots up. Chomp! The shark snatches up its next meal.

A mako shark has a giant mouth and sharp teeth.

A shortfin mako like this is much easier to find than a longfin mako.

 How big can mako sharks grow?

There are two types of makos darting around the ocean. Shortfins are the most common. Longfins are harder to find. And yes, longfins have longer fins. But there are other differences. Longfins have larger eyes. Their **snouts** are also darker. But they swim so fast, you might not be able to see the difference.

 Up to 13 feet (4 m) long. That's about as long as two grown-up people.

Makos are built for speed. They have thin, **streamlined** bodies. They have strong, curved tails. With a flick of their tails, they shoot through the water. They are one of the fastest sharks in the sea. Makos can swim up to 40 miles per hour (64 kph). They use their quickness to catch **prey**.

A mako is shaped like a rocket. It can swim fast!

People can see mako sharks near this California beach.

 Q How do scientists know where makos go during the year?

Mako sharks live in most of the world's oceans. They swim in the Pacific and Atlantic Oceans. They live in the Indian Ocean. In the summer, makos are found in colder areas. But in winter, makos **migrate** to warmer water. Scientists are not exactly sure why they move from place to place.

 They use tags. People catch sharks and put tags on them. The tag sends information to computers about where the sharks go.

Dinner Time

Like all sharks, makos eat meat. They gulp
down almost anything they can catch.
Makos often feed on fish that live in
schools. This way, makos can snatch up
a bunch of fish at once. They also hunt
big fish. These can include swordfish and
smaller sharks. Squid, dolphins, and turtles
can become mako meals, too.

It's a shark buffet! Makos eat turtles and schools of fish.

The mako's teeth are like sharp hooks that snag their food.

 How does a mako eat big fish?

Mako sharks have rows and rows of teeth. Their teeth are long and thin. They are hooked and angle inward. They are good for gripping slippery fish. Once a mako shark bites onto a fish, the prey will squirm and thrash. But it won't be able to get away. Now it's dinner!

 Sometimes, a mako bites the tail off a big fish. This keeps it from swimming away.

Life Cycle

Scientists do not know much about how mako sharks **mate**. It is believed they mate in the summer and fall. This might be why they migrate. They give birth more than a year later.

Makos give **live birth** to their young. Young sharks are called **pups**. Most females have 8 to 10 pups. They swim away after giving birth.

Two sharks come together to mate. The mother gives birth to live pups more than a year later.

Both young and old mako sharks swim near the surface of the water.

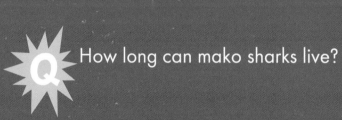

How long can mako sharks live?

Young mako sharks look like small **adults**. They are about 28 inches (70 cm) long. Like most shark pups, they can swim well and hunt for food right away. Makos grow slowly. It takes about 18 years for females to reach adulthood. Males become adults around 8 years of age.

 About 30 years.

Life as a Predator

A mako shark has a blue-gray color on its back. Some have a deep indigo color. But this color is more than just for show. It helps the mako blend in with the ocean floor. Fish cannot see it swimming from above. Watch out, fish! A mako might be lurking below!

The mako's white belly helps it blend in with the sun from below.

A mako's eyes and nose are
perfect for finding food.

 Can other animals sense electricity
like the mako can?

Mako sharks find prey with their senses. They can hear and smell. Makos have large eyes for a shark. They can see prey better than some other sharks can. Makos also have a sense that we do not have. They can detect electricity. All animals give off small bits of energy when they move. Makos can sense this energy. It helps them find their prey.

 Yes. Sharks and rays have this ability. So do platypuses and bees!

Mako sharks do something most sharks don't do. They leap out of the water. They can jump 20 feet (6 m) into the air. Why? Scientists are not sure. Some think it helps them catch prey. These sharks can do this because they are not like most other fish. Makos are warm-blooded. They can keep their bodies warmer than the water they swim in. This helps them move better.

Not many sharks leap out of the water like a mako shark does.

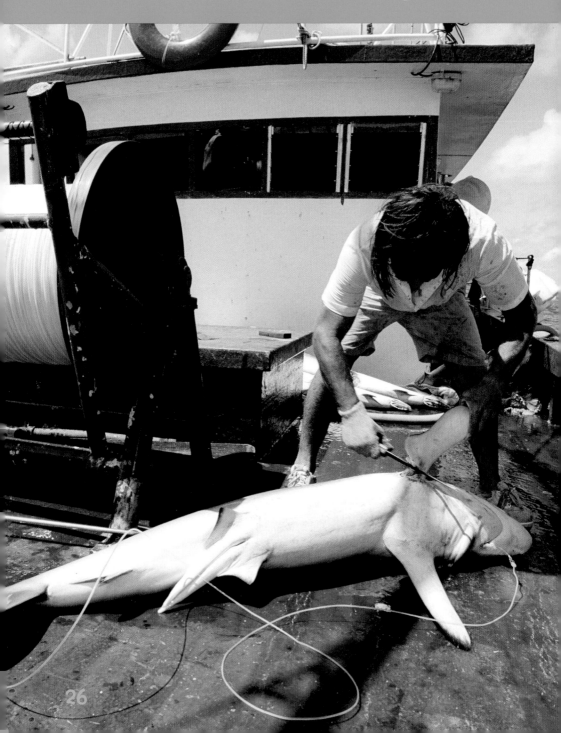

A fisher cuts a fin off of a young mako shark. He might use the fins to make shark fin soup.

Mako Sharks and People

Mako sharks can be dangerous. Like other sharks, makos do not try to eat people. But sometimes they mistake a swimmer for a seal or a turtle. Mako attacks are rare.

People are more dangerous to makos. People use shark liver oil to make medicine. Some governments have passed laws. The laws limit the number of makos that can be caught.

People like to go fishing in the ocean. This is a problem for makos. The fish makos eat might be gone. The good news is that mako sharks will eat lots of different foods. If people work to keep the world's oceans **diverse**, these speedsters will keep swimming.

A diver uses an underwater camera to take pictures of a stunning mako shark.

Glossary

adult A fully-grown animal.

diverse Having many different kinds and varieties.

live birth When a mother gives birth to babies rather than laying eggs.

mate To pair up to produce young.

migrate To move from one area to another in a pattern.

prey Animals eaten as food by other animals.

pup A young shark.

snout The part of an animal's head where the nose and mouth are.

streamlined Designed to move through air or water more easily.

Read More

Gray, Susan H. *Mako Sharks*. Ann Arbor, Mich: Cherry Lake Pub., 2014.

Green, Sara. *The Mako Shark*. Minneapolis: Bellwether Media, Inc., 2012.

Musgrave, Ruth. *National Geographic Kids Everything Sharks*. Washington, D.C.: National Geographic, 2011.

Websites

Arkive—Longfin Mako Shark
www.arkive.org/longfin-mako/isurus-paucus/

Discovery Channel—Shortfin Mako Shark
www.discovery.com/tv-shows/shark-week/types-of-shark/shortfin-mako-shark

Shark Sider—Shortfin Mako Shark
www.sharksider.com/shortfin-mako-shark/

Index

About the Author

Allan Morey is a children's book author and loves animals, both big and small. He's had pet fish, birds, ferrets, pigs, cats, and dogs. Animals are one of his favorite subjects to write about. He now lives in St. Paul, Minnesota, with his wife, two kids, and dog, Ty.

5